See, Love, Lift

How Seeing, Loving, and Lifting Others

Will Change Your Life

Jason F. Wright

UNION BRIDGE BOOKS

See, Love, Lift — *How Seeing, Loving, and Lifting Others Will Change Your Life*

© 2020 Jason F. Wright
© 2020 Union Bridge Books

ISBN: 978-0-578-24106-7

www.jasonfwright.com

Jason Wright
Wright Media Enterprises
Post Office Box 669
Woodstock, Virginia 22664

Other Books by Jason F. Wright

For Aaron "Al" Lee

Al's rare ability to see, love, and lift others has been an inspiration in my life for more than twenty years.

If you're ever blessed to meet my friend, please ask him about our road trip to New York City in 2004.

Praise for *See, Love, Lift*

"This book changed my attitude and lifted my spirits. It answered a prayer on how I can minister to others. My prayers will be different now. I will pray to see. As my attitude changes, my prayers will change, my actions will change and then my heart and soul will be uplifted. Thank you for a life changing experience!"

—*LeAnn Lash*
Madison, Alabama

"As Jason reflected on his life, it was as if I were observing the events and how they can make a difference in who we may become. All along we are given the opportunity to plan how we can make a difference. All ages will be able to gift these rights to those in our lives."

—*Gwenda Tucker*
Oxnard, California

"If we could commit to seeing, loving, and lifting—just once—there would be less hate, loneliness, and selfishness in the world. I'm truly more enlightened from having read this."

—*Tracy Rine*
Glen Easton, West Virginia

"During this period of physical and emotional isolation, Jason reminds us of our undiminished power to bless others by truly seeing, loving, and lifting them up, even in simple ways."

—*Megan Taylor*
Lehi, Utah

"This short but eloquent booklet starts right from the beginning getting me to think about my relationship with those around me, those I know and those who I should get to know. How can I see better? How do I show love? How can I lift others in ways that will help them know they are a child of God? Hopefully I can be better, and maybe, so can the world around me.

—Becky Ellefson Sprague
Richmond, Indiana

"Several years ago, I was promoted into a manager position. It was only after I accepted the position that the director informed me that I was inheriting the worst team in that area. Within a year it was one of the best within the entire company. Folks asked what my secret was. This book sums it up perfectly. See what they need. Love them as the individuals they are. Lift them up with recognition and appreciation."

—Kurt Karafinski
Pittsburgh, Pennsylvania

"I felt moved to tears at the thought of those who simply long for a hug and to hear the words 'I love you,' something many of us take for granted, yet something so simple. This was a great reminder that some of the greatest service we can render to our brothers and sisters is often small and simple."

—*Santyna Johnstone-Arnold*
Estacada, Oregon

"See, Love, Lift has inspired me to view those around me in a new way and to improve how I interact with others! I love the space provided after each section to make notes about impressions. I can't wait to put my new impressions into action! Jason's new book is a worthwhile read!"

—*Deanna Christensen*
Kearneysville, West Virginia

See, Love, Lift

Introduction

Why am I writing this?

Because inspiration often visits me at night.

There's something so special about the still of the house and the glow from tiny bulbs in night lights and bright, boxy numbers on alarm clocks.

Whether it's been for my spiritual, family, personal, or professional life, many of my most memorable ideas have come when the people and the home that I love are sleeping.

It never lasts too long, but for a few magical moments, it's just me, my imagination, and heaven.

In March of 2017, I was preparing for an unusual early morning speaking engagement in a northern Virginia suburb. I'd been invited to address a gathering of about fifty high schoolers who choose to attend a Bible study class—often called seminary—each day before school.

I spent hours that week pondering, organizing thoughts, and jotting down straggly notes. The night before the event, I went to bed feeling mild confidence that I had something interesting and valuable to share.

Then, it happened.

I woke up in the middle of the night and met either inspiration or indigestion face to face.

Either way, I felt prompted to scrap what I had prepared and to start fresh.

Before I could even rub the sleep from my eyes, three phrases scrolled through my mind like starring credits at the start of a movie. I stared at the ceiling and processed this middle-of-the-night flash.

After a few minutes of peace, I reached over to my nightstand and fetched my phone. Then I opened my notes app and, with my eyes squinting from the blinding light of my display, tapped out a phrase with my fat thumbs.

"We all come to earth with three divine rights. We have a right to be *seen*; we have a right to be *loved*; we have a right to be *lifted*."

I read the words back several times before powering down the phone and powering down my mind.

I wasn't so successful with the latter.

Eventually, I made my way to the shower, to my closet, to my kitchen, to my car, and to my commitment about fifty miles from home.

With the green Virginia hills rolling by, I outlined some remarks using Siri on that same phone that bailed me out in the middle of the night. Soon, I walked into the room with little more than some instinct and a few stories.

It's always hard to know how well received you are as a speaker. But I admit I drove home feeling hopeful that I'd delivered the message heaven and my imagination had intended. Maybe more importantly, I realized the message might have been more for me than for those sleepy-eyed teenagers.

As the weeks and months marched by, I spent a lot of time pondering those three phrases.

What might they mean in my life?

Or in the lives of the people I love, worship with, and work with each and every day?

I've since spoken about the concept many times in other venues—both religious and secular.

When I'm speaking to church groups, I tend to focus on the spiritual blessings of embracing these concepts and what I believe with all my heart are the heavenly truths that drive these divine rights.

When I'm in school, corporate, or conference settings, I focus on the global, practical benefits of living our lives this way. I like to remind audiences of all kinds that kindness doesn't care what church you go to.

May we all remember that when tragedy, depression, loneliness, sickness, or simple sadness strikes, our neighbors in need don't check the status of our testimonies at the door.

Regardless of what the speaking engagements look like, or whether I'm staring at a few or a thousand faces, each time I dive into this notion of divine rights,

I seem to better understand why I had the impressions that night in the first place.

Perhaps that's why I'm writing this little book. Because more than anyone I've ever known, I have so much to learn about the need to better *see*, *love*, and *lift* others.

Maybe, just maybe, we'll learn something together.

Part One

Seen

Ask any child who's been through America's school system, and hopefully the adults in your life, and they should know something about the Constitution and our inspired Bill of Rights. Most know we have a right to life, liberty, and the pursuit of happiness.

These rights might have come from the pens of men. But many, including myself, believe they originate in a place that we cannot see, by a perfect God we cannot truly comprehend.

What we talk much less about in schools, churches, or the workplace, are the rights we have that are more difficult to define, but that can become the foundation of our daily journey.

Christians often speak about being the hands of the Lord to do His work here on earth.

Why do we open a door for someone whose arms are full, or who simply needs an extra hand?

Why do we stop and change a tire for someone in need, in the rain on the side of the road, who seems to be struggling on their own?

Why do we physically give a hug to someone in tears when there's no doubt that same person is receiving unseen spiritual hugs from ministering angels?

Because if we seek to be disciples of Christ, then we truly are His tangible, seeable, imperfect hands in an imperfect world. I have no doubt this principle is true and should be promoted every time and every place we can.

But what if we're missing step one?

How can we be the *hands* of the Lord, on earth, to do His work, if we're not the *eyes* of the Lord to see the opportunities?

How can we use our hands to open a physical door if our eyes don't first see our neighbor's needs?

How can we change a tire if we're driving so fast down the highway, looking straight ahead and never trusting our peripheral vision, that we don't even *see* the person perhaps praying for help?

How can we know to be the hands or, in this case, the arms of the Lord to literally embrace one of our earthly brothers or sisters in pain if our eyes aren't looking up and in every direction for those desperately searching for someone?

We can't.

It's impossible to be the hands of the Lord unless we are first His eyes. When Jesus Christ sent His disciples out to teach, to minister, and to love as He taught them, they did much with their hands.

They prayed, they taught, they wrote, they witnessed. And they did all this because their eyes were open to see those around them.

Today any leader in any faith—whether Christian, Jewish, or some other—cannot care for their members or congregants with their hands unless their eyes are open during worship services, sermons, Sunday schools, or perhaps while working at the food bank, to see the opportunities heaven is placing in front of them.

When I was young, my family lived in Germany for five years. This was an interesting time in our family history and, while I don't remember nearly as much as my three older siblings, I remember how close we were as a family and how deeply my parents loved one another and each one of us.

I remember witnessing my father's knack for seeing people around him and around our family. One day, as the family rode along in our station wagon, my father somehow spotted a woman off the edge of the road attempting to get into a small boat. Dad hit the brakes, safely pulled the car off the road and, as he'd done before and would do many times later, disappeared to put his hands to work.

We later learned that the woman had decided to go out into the boat to be independent and to go for a short sail she thought she could handle. But being alone and inexperienced, she'd quickly grown afraid.

My father took her by the hand, led her to safety and, while I don't know if he said the words or not, he clearly sent the message that she was not alone. He'd seen her and he served her.

When my sister recalls this memory, she remembers our father returning the car and describing the woman as being *frozen*. I've often wondered how many people around us each day are frozen in fear, uncertainly, or loneliness.

Are *you* the one that frozen soul needs to take her by the physical or spirit hand?

Years later, my father passed away a week before Christmas during my junior year of high school. That was, of course, the greatest trial of my life, and I'm not embarrassed to share that it took me longer than most to recover and rebuild.

Losing parents at any age is difficult. Losing a parent at sixteen—and being the youngest at the time—seemed unjust.

Because my father's passing and funeral were so close to the Christmas break, I didn't return to school until after the New Year. Even then, I told my mother that I didn't quite feel ready, and I asked for another week to regroup at home.

She didn't love the idea, but she did love me. So, we negotiated that if I would go into the school to get some work from my teachers to do at home to stay busy, and to begin to catch up, she would give me another few days off.

I'll never forget putting on my dad's long wool overcoat and riding with my mother to Albemarle High School in Charlottesville, Virginia. I wondered aloud to my mother how many of the students in our large high school had any idea what had happened.

Do they know?

Do they care?

Have they noticed I've been out of school since the week before break began?

Will they say anything to me?

Will they even *see* me?

My mother pulled up in front of the main entrance and waited as I disappeared through the front door. It was lunchtime, and there were kids buzzing about the hallways, heading in every possible direction. I cut a path through them toward an upstairs classroom where my English teacher had gathered up work from my other teachers into a thick manila envelope.

I remember walking in and interrupting her chatting casually with several other students who smiled and nodded. I remember her hugging me and telling me how sorry she was, and how excited she would be to have me back in class.

I smiled back, and I don't remember if I said much, but I've always hoped she felt my deep gratitude for her concern.

I turned to move back down the hallway and walked toward the stairs that would lead me to the front doors and to my mother's car. As I weaved through a gaggle of students, a beautiful young lady startled me when she called me by name. I believe she was a senior and that it was the first time she'd spoken to me.

Honestly? I was pleasantly surprised she knew I even existed.

She tugged on the sleeve of the overcoat that drowned me and I turned to meet her eyes. Leaning in slightly, eyes locked on mine, she said in the softest and sweetest voice I'd ever heard, "Jason, are you okay?"

Tears flooded my eyes and I softly nodded. Then I turned away, quickly shuffled down the stairs and out the door. I remember dropping into the passenger seat of my mother's car and finally letting the tears flow freely.

I told her what happened and how surprised I was that a girl I didn't know, and who I didn't think knew me, had looked me right in the eyes to say four words that meant so much more.

She'd seen me, I thought.

In a sea of students, self-absorbed and worried about 1,001 other things, she'd somehow *seen* me. And because she'd *seen* me, she'd been able to *serve* me.

And because she'd *served* me, I felt *loved*.

Years later, I still don't know her name, but I do know that if she stopped me in a grocery store aisle, or in a church hallway, or in an airport terminal, I'd know her face.

I'd know her eyes.

Just three years later, I served a volunteer mission for The Church of Jesus Christ of Latter-day Saints in Minas Gerais, Brazil and my first area was the small but stunning city of Sete Lagoas. I'd only been in the country a few days and, though I felt prepared to leave home and spend two years doing God's work, I found myself lost and homesick on my first morning in my first assignment.

After getting up at 6:30, eating breakfast and tackling daily studies, I learned from the other missionaries in our apartment that we'd been asked to assist some other local church members in doing light landscaping at the soccer field adjacent to our chapel. They were preparing for an upcoming tournament and wanted the field to look its best.

I walked along with seven other young men approximately my age but all of whom had more time in the country. When we arrived at the soccer field, we were given assignments and scattered out within eyesight of one another to begin weeding, raking, and preparing the field.

I don't recall how long we'd been there when I wandered off to a corner, still within sight and sound of the other missionaries, and sat in a small patch of grass. I pulled up dandelions and other weeds and tossed them to the side.

Like rainstorms that arrive from nowhere and drench cities in South America, I felt a wave of emotion crash down on me. I was thousands of miles from home—with no idea where I really was in the country—and I felt completely disoriented and discombobulated. I picked at the weeds until I was staring at a bare, brown spot of dirt.

A few minutes later, one of the other missionaries noticed me and slowly made his way over to sit by my side. I explained that I knew I'd be all right, but that I felt out of place in this new city, in this new country, sitting in a soccer field, melting under the blistering sun, and praying for some way to find my inner compass.

This young man, an American who'd been out on his mission for more than a year, found a short stick and drew a map in the dirt. I remember him specifically pointing out where we were in relation to São Paulo, where we were in relation to our mission headquarters in the city of Belo Horizonte, and where I was in relation to my hometown of Charlottesville.

Suddenly, in a patch of dirt, the world took shape and I felt calm chase away the storm.

Soon I was on my feet and feeling optimistic about my new challenges, my new friends, this language I had faith I'd learn, and this strange country I would almost immediately fall in love with.

Oh, how I fell in love with Brazil! The people, the language, the culture, and the memories are all etched into my heart. And while I loved every city and every family I met, that first assignment—Sete Lagoas—holds an extra special place in my heart. I long to walk her streets again, to hug the people who became like family, and *see* as many people as I possibly can.

That soccer field experience was maybe thirty minutes and more than thirty years ago. But I remember it with such clarity with my emotional eyes, because I'd been *seen*.

This other young man had to open his eyes and, with clear vision and a desire to serve, became the hands and voice of the Lord.

Now, it's obvious that I might have recovered from that lonely morning on my own. Maybe I would have bounced back and been able to get my feet under me by lunchtime and gone on to have the same kind of wonderful experience in Brazil.

But the lesson I learned that hot day in Sete Lagoas was that I hadn't had to recover all alone, because someone had been watching.

I've spent the years since trying to spot other people sitting alone in the corner of life's fields praying someone would see them.

And, I pray, helping them know who and where they are.

Decades after that experience with my father and the woman in Germany, I found history repeating itself. I've wondered, lately, if it's because the lesson had only been half taught or—perhaps more accurately—only half learned.

Four years ago, I was driving my boys thirty miles to the south of our home in Woodstock, Virginia to the city of Harrisonburg to run a few errands and to play a long overdue round of mini-golf. As we kept up with traffic on the always crammed Interstate 81—flying somewhere between seventy and eighty miles an hour—my oldest son, Kason, shouted that he saw a goat stuck in a fence at a farm to our right.

By the time I understood what he was suggesting and could look behind me, the property was out of sight, and the goat in the fence was just a memory that I strongly suspected was fiction from an imaginative, storytelling kid.

I turned to Kason with a sly smile and said, "You've got to be kidding me, right kiddo? At this speed, surrounded by semi-trucks, you saw a goat whose horns were stuck in a fence up a hill?"

He was insistent and convinced his brother in the backseat that, not only was he right, but that we had a moral obligation to turn around at the next exit, and to drive back to see if we could help.

I made a playful bet that there'd be no goat flailing in a fence and that going back would only cost all of us time and him a pound of pride.

Doubtful, but always up for an adventure, I indeed flipped around at the next exit, drove all the way back past the spot that was not visible because of tall trees in median, then turned around again for an opportunity to set the record straight.

Eventually we pulled safely well off the road at the spot he guaranteed would reveal a goat in need of saving.

Sure enough, there it was.

Just as Kason described, a short distance from the interstate and up a steep hill, a goat was thrashing around with his horns caught in the fence that kept him and his goat pals safe from the road.

We traipsed up the hill and, after a phone call to their mother who grew up with goats on a ranch in Wyoming, my sons freed their new friend. Before we left, the owner saw us and came to say thank you.

My son enjoyed being right. And by 'enjoyed,' I mean that he relished every second of the remainder of that drive, and the episode cost me an extra scoop of post mini-golf ice cream and, perhaps, a dash of credibility.

As the story was retold later at home, and later to friends, I couldn't help but reminisce on my own father recognizing that you should never be driving or living too fast to see needs from your peripheral vision.

We could have never been the hands to serve the goat if we hadn't been the eyes to *see* the goat.

We all know it's true, don't we? We live in a hyperactive world where speed is everything. Nothing can stream, run, drive, download, or deliver fast enough to satisfy us. And that's precisely why it's more important than ever that we do more than simply look up from our devices and distractions. We must also look left and right—literally and spiritually—to see all of God's children.

Imagine a paradigm shift where every one of us recognized that by simply being alive on this earth—no matter our race, our gender, our age, or our lifestyle—we have a divine right to be seen.

Imagine if no one in your community ever felt alone, if no one ever felt invisible.

Imagine if worth and the right to be seen wasn't determined by zip code, tax returns, or heritage.

I'm not suggesting that every problem can be solved by helping someone across a bridge, or drawing a map in the dirt, or from freeing a goat from a fence.

No, but I am suggesting that life's most delicious and healthy solutions are made from individual ingredients that always start with *one*. And that *one* must be that we see *one* another, value *one* another without question or hesitation, and we respect *one* another's right to see . . . and be seen.

How Can I Better *See*
Someone Today?

_____

_____

_____

_____

_____

_____

_____

_____

_____

_____

_____

_____

_____

_____

_____

People I Will Share This
Principle With Today

_____

_____

_____

_____

_____

_____

_____

_____

_____

_____

_____

_____

_____

_____

Part Two

Loved

I'm so grateful to have grown up in home, community, and church families where I never felt a lack of *love*. I was raised to believe that love is a verb. It is an action word and not simply some idea that floats around in space and, occasionally, lands on an overpriced greeting card.

Ask any wife how she wants to be loved by her husband. She'll tell you that hearing the word as she walks out the door is important, but seeing the word in action is so much more critical.

Husbands and wives crave to see the word *love* in everything their spouse does.

If you're a husband, and you question whether your wife really thinks that showing love means doing dishes or taking trash out, just ask her. Every member of a family longs to witness love in action all day, every day.

When my father passed away, I had many people express and demonstrate love in disparate ways. But looking back, one has always stood out above the rest. The teacher who gathered up homework for me that day I returned to the high school was Charlotte Wellen. Mrs. Wellen taught English, Creative Writing, and was the Forensics speech coach.

She was also a friend to everyone who walked into her classroom, and her faith in the students she taught is the reason many of them survived—not just high school, but adolescence.

I knew she loved me and never doubted she believed in me. But a few days after my father's death, just after the funeral, she slipped an envelope into my hand.

Later, in a private place, I opened it up to find a handwritten letter on yellow legal-sized paper in her distinctive handwriting that I'd seen many times before. The letter told me that though we might have different beliefs about God and heaven, she knew both were real. And that she knew one day I'd see him again, and that until then, he'd be closer than I knew.

The letter promised me that if I stayed true to my beliefs, if I continued to learn, to grow, and to love, that I'd find happiness again. And that the clouds that suffocated me would thin out and eventually dissipate.

I cried when I read the letter, and I've cried many times since when rereading or even thinking of it. Even today, I know just where the letter is and I've read it more times than I could count. The letter was love in action, and I feel loved all over again every single time I read it.

What I love most about being a writer is less sitting at a desk and scrambling to put words in some interesting order, and much more standing in front of students, in public and private schools, and speaking to them on themes and principles I think could improve their journey to adulthood.

I've spoken to many thousands of students, from kindergarten through high school, in almost every state in the country. Often, teachers and administrators who bring me in arrange for me to have lunch with a pre-selected group of students.

Sometimes, it's students who love to write. Other times it's the students in leadership positions within the school. And, sometimes, it's students who are so far off the radar, they rarely appear on anyone's screen. This is my favorite group.

We sit around a small table and I can usually look into their eyes and discern something simple about their home life. It's dangerous to stereotype, of course, and generalizations sometimes get us all into trouble. But it's easy to tell why many of these young people were selected for this kind of an experience.

We often share a catered lunch the schools so generously provide. It might be as simple as sandwiches, chips, and giant chocolate chips. But invariably it's one of the nicest meals they can remember having. I'm always touched by how grateful and in awe they are to be treated like VIPs for a few minutes.

As we eat, laugh and linger, I ask them questions about their interests and hobbies and dreams and habits.

What do they like to do?

Where do they like to go?

What do they want to be when grow up?

More importantly, *who* do they want to be when they grow up?

When the answers come too slowly, I really probe. What's their favorite thing to do when there are no restrictions on their time or choices, and they can be their own agents to act, with no one standing in the way?

I am always a blend of surprised and saddened when their answers are tied to family. Naturally, it's wonderful that they would want to spend time with their mom or their dad or their grandma or their great uncle. But time and time again in these discussions, I hear how infrequently these memories are actually made with family and how rarely they feel loved.

That last line bears repeating—how rarely they feel loved.

On a few occasions, I've gone a step further and asked, "When is the last time someone at home said, 'I love you?' Or gave you a hug? Or better yet, when was the last time someone did both?"

Not long ago in a population of particularly troubled students—who come from backgrounds, in some cases, so unbelievable they feel like fiction—I asked those questions and braced for a response. At least half in the conference room where we gathered could not remember the last time a family member looked them in the eye and expressed love.

When I asked if there are people in their lives who demonstrate love but aren't good at saying it, the answers were similar. And when I asked point blank, "Does your mother love you? Does your stepfather love you? Does your grandmother love you? Does your older brother or sister love you?"

The students looked back at me, some choking back emotions they wouldn't know how to articulate anyway, and each offered some variation of this tragic line. "I . . . have no idea."

As difficult as these lunchtime discussions can be, they open my eyes to the need of all people at all ages to hear and feel and sense and be wrapped up in love.

Yes, those young people in that classroom probably make their share of mistakes. Sometimes, even when easy to love, they might be difficult to like. Many might struggle with authority or rules or order.

And maybe they behave as though all they know or care about is chaos, but none of that excuses those around them from their responsibility to live love.

One of my last trips before COVID-19 blew up our calendars and careers took me to another elementary school in an impoverished part of the country. I'm used to kids saying "thank you" and "goodbye" and wanting high fives and hugs as they stream out of an auditorium or a cafeteria at the end of my presentations. One little girl approached me with a hope in her eyes that I hadn't seen before.

I had just spoken about how magical these children were, how bright their futures are, and how much I believe in them and will always believe in them— even if no one else in their life will. It's something I say often because I really believe it. I want to be, if nothing else, the one adult that day or that week or that month or that year, who unequivocally promises to always have faith in their ability to achieve.

This exchange, however, was different.

This student with thin blonde hair that needed both a wash and a cut slowly drifted out of her classroom line toward me with her arms outstretched.

I see the moment so clearly.

I knelt down to give her a hug while her teacher smiled from across the hall. As the girl pulled away, she looked at me and said, "I love you, Mr. Wright."

My heart broke.

I wonder how long it had been since anyone had said those words back to her.

So, of course, I did.

Yes, I said "I love you" to a girl I'll probably never see again, but whom I'll never forget.

For the rest of my life, when I think about this particular divine right, I will always think of that angelic girl, her sweet face, and her longing to be cared for.

And her desperate desire to be truly loved.

How Can I Better *Love*

Someone Today?

_____

_____

_____

_____

_____

_____

_____

_____

_____

_____

_____

_____

_____

_____

_____

People I Will Share This

Principle With Today

_____

_____

_____

_____

_____

_____

_____

_____

_____

_____

_____

_____

_____

_____

Part Three

Lifted

Do you remember the first time you went to your mom or dad with a crayon drawing that was mostly outside the lines?

Or maybe it was a clay sheep that didn't look anything like an actual sheep. Or was it that macaroni necklace painted and carefully covered with tissue paper for Mother's Day?

And do you remember what their response was when you presented them with this magnificent piece of art? Odds are you were met with something like this.

"This is beautiful! You are *so* talented! You made this all by yourself? You are such a gifted artist."

Lies, lies, and more lies, right?

From the beginning of our lives, as far back as we can remember, people around us elevate us—they *lift* us to a place where we don't yet belong.

They tell us how fast we are in our brand new tennis shoes.

They tell us how beautiful the music is that we make on that ninety-nine-cent recorder that they'd like to strap fireworks to and blow up in the backyard.

Wonderful teachers, wise parents, thoughtful coaches look for opportunities to lift those in their care and stewardship to a higher station. It builds self-esteem and creates a sense of hope.

I've written before about my earliest memories as a writer, and I'm not talking about the struggling days as a professional writer making the jump from my previous careers. I'm referring to the early years as a child writing in my room past midnight. And when I wasn't creating worlds with a pen or pencil, I was creating them in my head.

My favorite early memory is a story I tell often in schools and at conferences. I share it so frequently because I recognize decades later that the memory isn't important to me because it was entertaining, but because it changed me and has become one of the anchor memories of my life.

The story swirls around a wonderful third grade teacher who had a knack for believing that every single one of her students could become something. Now, that *something* was obviously going to be very different for each one of us. But every single day that I walked into her classroom, I felt as though I were walking

41

into a dream factory where no one ever snickered if you wanted to play in the NFL.

No one mocked you if you said you wanted to be a movie star. No one pointed their finger and giggled if you said one day you wanted to be a *New York Times* bestselling writer.

I mean, they didn't even know what that was. But *I* did, and I knew that I wanted to learn to become one.

On a Friday, our teacher pulled several students aside to a small table in the back of our classroom. We'd been studying different types of writing for a couple of weeks—poetry, short stories, and simple book reports. She explained that we wouldn't have time as a class to learn how to write skits or plays but that she wanted our group to have that experience. She knew that we always gravitated toward opportunities to write early and often and promised us that it would be worth a little extra effort to learn the art.

She very simply taught what a skit might look like and what format she would expect. Character names, action, a little dialogue—it was all very . . . elementary. We were thrilled, and she even promised we could act a few of them out.

I sat at my little desk and wrote a play called *Molly and Polly*. It was about two bunny rabbits who wore leather jackets, rode Harleys, and solved crime. I certainly don't want to overstate it, so I'll be careful here, but it was probably the greatest five-page play in the history of American literature.

I remember taking it back to her desk and standing as she quickly read it. I watched so eagerly as she placed her hands upon it as if to bless it, then turned to look me in the eye. She said, "Jason, this is really good. You should do more of this." A light bulb went off in my head like a massive mushroom cloud, and I can't confirm that I heard angels singing somewhere in the back of my head. (I did.)

I rushed home after school and spent the weekend writing in my room. I remember successfully swiping and eating a full box of oatmeal cream pies from the pantry and hoping my mom wouldn't notice. But, if she did, I'd have an excuse that she couldn't counter. I was in my room *writing*.

I came out of hibernation on Monday morning in a bathrobe, six inches taller and sporting a long beard. I must have had a pencil tucked back behind my ear and some oatmeal cream pie tagging along in the hair under my chin.

I went to school with a stack of *Molly and Polly* plays and rushed to see my teacher. I plopped the stack down and said, "Here you go!"

She looked at me a bit confused and said, "Oh, good morning. What is this?"

I answered her with a smile that reappears every time I remember the moment. "It's a whole *series* of Molly and Polly plays."

44

She smiled back and said, "Wait, why?"

"Well, you told me to do *more* of this."

She tousled my hair and said, "Oh Jason, I didn't mean so soon."

If I was deflated, it couldn't have lasted long. The next thing I remember she'd offered to read every word on every page and to give me feedback.

True to her word, she did, and I pestered her each day to see how she liked the next one.

I also remember that a week or two later the assistant principal poked her head into our classroom during homeroom. I didn't know her well, but her face was friendly and she seemed kind.

Everyone noticed, of course, that our principal had stepped a few feet into the room. Then she caught my eye and said in front of the entire class, "Mr. Wright, I read one of your plays. It was awesome!"

Then she gave me a thumbs up and finished a quick conversation with our teacher before walking out.

If unicorns and flying monkeys had crashed into the closed classroom windows, I wouldn't have noticed. I could have floated up like a magic carpet on my desk and all the way home.

Naturally, I told my parents the story later that day, and they lovingly reinforced the goodness these educators had showered on me. Let's call this precisely what it was. It was a lift.

Was I writing great prose in elementary school?

Was I crafting scenes that would land on Broadway?

Of course not. But she'd made me feel as though I were a great writer.

Now this teacher and many after her would be hard on me; I was grateful for that too. They didn't simply tell me that everything I produced was flawless and that I'd never need to pick up a red pen to make something better. They pushed me to work harder, to dive a little deeper when I thought I was done, and to never stop improving.

But even then, when the quality wasn't what it should be and they challenged me to be better, I always felt like they were lifting me to a level that I didn't yet belong in, but that one day I would.

You might be interested to know that not long after that first experience with Molly and Polly, I wrote an 11-page edition called *Molly and Polly's First Christmas*. It was, once again, a page-turner for the ages. I swiped a few stamps from my mother's desk and sent it to a publisher in New York.

Before long, I received a postcard back in the mail telling me that my submission had been forwarded on to the publishing committee for consideration.

I didn't know at the time that it was nothing more than a form letter to convey they'd received it. I thought there was a legitimate chance I'd be getting my first publishing deal! Molly and Polly were about to go global!

I'm happy to report that as of 2020, I have not heard back. Perhaps it's still under consideration?

A few years later, I was at church on a Sunday morning preparing to pass the sacrament for the first time. I was so nervous!

Sacrament, of course, means broken bread and water. They are the emblems of the body and blood of Christ.

Fine, maybe *terrified* is a more accurate word.

One of my best friends, Jose, was also passing the sacrament for the first time and we tried to comfort one another. We were like two rookie ball players finally taking the field and sharing all they knew— and all they really didn't.

Somehow we managed to successfully pass the bread and water throughout the congregation with several other boys without incident.

When we were done and the service ended, one of our youth leaders, Barry McLerram, approached and asked if he could speak to us privately for a minute. My friend and I were sure we had done something wrong and were about to be reprimanded. Or worse! Fired?

He pulled us aside, and with a hand on one of my shoulders and one on Jose's, he told us that he'd been watching us closely. He wanted us to know that he'd noticed how reverent we were and how dignified we were in approaching our responsibilities.

I remember Jose and I slowly making our way to Sunday school and thinking, *what just happened?*

Had he seen the same thing we had?

The reality of our first attempt passing the sacrament was changed in less than 60 seconds. We went from embarrassed and shy to talk about how we'd fumbled our way through it, to standing tall and feeling some righteous pride that someone had noticed our best effort.

We got better, of course, and looked for ways to improve. Years later, I'm pleased that I always tried to treat that responsibility with dignity.

I think I can trace it all back to a conversation in a quiet hallway where someone saw an opportunity to lift Jose and me to a higher level, a place perhaps we didn't deserve yet, but that one day would.

This principle of the lift is evident in so many parts of life. A first-time NFL coach takes the field and in most cases is hardly ready to lead a billion-dollar team in front of millions of people watching on TV. But we lift them; we trust them. We tell them they're the best coach in the league and how grateful we are to have them on our side.

Actors, actresses, musicians, and other artists often get that big role, or that big opportunity, or that big break long before they're ready. But because someone says, "I believe you'll be great. Here's your chance to become so."

I sometimes think of a graduate from seminary or theological school somewhere landing their first position in a church. A congregation sits and awaits all his or her wisdom and scriptural insights.

That pastor or minister probably isn't the greatest speaker, teacher, or scriptorian to be found, but church members will treat him or her that way.

They will lift, love, and expect great things And as they do, more often than not, that man or woman of God will rise up.

Can you remember the last time that you stopped to spiritually, or emotionally, or even physically, lift someone?

I assure you that today someone will walk by you at work, or on the street, or in the store, or maybe in the hallway of your own home, feeling lonely, hopeless, or heavy.

They're begging you for a lift, for some faith, for some good news, for some confidence, for a few minutes of your time, or for a compliment.

There's yet another kind of lift I've discovered over the last few years. It's giving rides in my car to hitchhikers and the homeless.

I've always been, perhaps foolishly, too risk-tolerant and have never had a problem giving rides to strangers.

A couple of years ago during such a ride, with conversation as entertaining as any I'd had in ages, I asked my two passengers if we could film the discussion and then share it on social media. These were two unique people living on the road for years, and who most folks would never have an opportunity to get to know, much less even meet for a second.

I edited a 30-minute conversation down to five or six and posted it online. I was pleasantly surprised at the reaction. My audience adored these people, even if they didn't always understand their life choices or circumstances. This led to other rides with the homeless, the hitchhikers, and the world's wanderers.

The theme that emerged through nearly every conversation was that our time together had little to do with getting from point A to point B, and much more about an *emotional* lift.

Many of these people that we pass by every day aren't just physically homeless or without a clear destination. They're without a spiritual home. Many have few friends, if any. Many go days at a time without another human being looking them in the eye and helping them to know they have value in the world no matter how they look, where they live, or what they smell like.

I've not given a ride to a single hitchhiker or homeless person who hasn't been incredibly gracious and thankful for our time together. Rarely do they ask for money, although I do typically offer them something at the end of our discussion as a thank you—but it's never expected.

I've even had occasions where the passengers in my car, and thus the stars of our videos, refuse money at the end, making it clear that they simply were looking forward to a few miles with some air conditioning on their faces and a new friend to talk to.

And friends they become!

I keep in touch with some of them and I've even had a few of them in the car more than once.

But I suppose what I've most learned from these lifts is that it would be naïve for me to think that I'm the one doing all the lifting. At the end of our conversations and rides, I haven't done some heroic act by spending time with them, buying them a cold drink, or moving them a few more miles down the highway to their next stop.

No, *I'm* the one who's being lifted.

Every time I say goodbye to one of these new friends, I feel better about the world. I feel better about my own life and my own circumstances. I'm more grateful for what I've been blessed with and I'm more aware of people around me and I pledge to do even better to *see* them.

I'm not suggesting that everyone start picking up hitchhikers and the homeless and driving them from one side of the country to the other.

I'm not even suggesting that it's appropriate or safe for anyone to stop on a park bench and have lengthy conversations with people who might be struggling with addiction or mental illness.

But I *am* inviting you to consider if there's more you can do to lift people on this journey who have less than you do financially, emotionally, and spiritually.

Is there something you can do today to lift another, give them value, worth and hope?

To connect them, even just for a few minutes, to the love that God has for them?

And if nothing comes of a discussion with one of my passengers than a simple reminder that God is real and that He loves them?

I'm perfectly content.

No matter how many rides I give, no matter how many lifts I offer, I'll never forget that with each experience, God is *lifting* me much more than I deserve.

How Can I Better *Lift*

Someone Today?

_____

_____

_____

_____

_____

_____

_____

_____

_____

_____

_____

_____

_____

_____

_____

People I Will Share This

Principle With Today

_____

_____

_____

_____

_____

_____

_____

_____

_____

_____

_____

_____

_____

_____

_____

Part Four

So, what?

Y ou might be arriving at this page and thinking to yourself that it's all too simple and cliché.

So, what?

So Jason often can't sleep a night and gets weird ideas looking at the ceiling. Big deal.

Or maybe you're thinking there are so many other rights seen and unseen, that there are countless things you need to work on, and that the things on your personal list should also be considered required for living the best kind of life.

Well, you'd be right.

But imagine for a moment if every single person we came in contact with every single day, at least for a moment, was *seen*, *loved*, and *lifted*.

It would change everything.

It would create a domino effect around the world.

People have bad days, bad weeks, bad years, bad relationships, bad jobs, and unexpected trials that will punch them in the gut. But during those turbulent times, your moment of *seeing* them, *loving* them, and *lifting* them just might be the anchor they hold onto to know they can make it through tomorrow.

Isn't that all we're trying to do?

Life is a series of 24-hour tests and each day we get out of bed and take another one.

Will we be kind?

Will we be productive?

Will we be generous?

Will we be polite?

Will we stand for what we believe in?

Will we seek to learn something new?

Will we dream?

Will we have courage?

Will we keep the courage even when we fall and the whole world seems to be watching?

Will we have just enough fuel in the tank to stand back up again and to stay on our feet a little bit longer the next time?

It is those moments where people *see* us, *love* us, and *lift* us that provide drops of fuel when it seems it's time to give up.

Finally, I believe these principles come from a Godly pattern that is undeniable. The Savior of the world *sees* us every single day.

He is aware of our needs, hears our prayers, and answers them on His time, and in His way, and with His wisdom.

No one is ever invisible to the perfect Lord of Lords.

Christ sees!

The same Christ loves us, and He loves us unconditionally. It doesn't mean that He doesn't weep when we make poor choices or wish we'd sometimes zig instead of zag. Of course, He does.

He didn't live an example of discipleship on the earth for us to simply read about and not to follow. He desires us to do all we can to be like Him, and then He promises that He will always make up the difference.

Maybe better put, He doesn't just make up the difference, He *is* the difference. He *is* the difference between a life that ends in the dust, or a life that lives forever in eternity at His side.

Christ loves!

Hasn't He also taught the principle of the lift since the beginning of time?

He asked fishermen to drop their nets and to follow Him. He asked sinners, thieves, and harlots to follow Him.

Christ, more than anyone in history, was lifted by His father, our Heavenly Father.

An unschooled, poor, humble boy was born to innocent parents without means, and the Father lifted Him to become the Savior of the world.

With no education, He was the most educated.

With no experience in leading, He was the greatest leader.

With no sin of His own, He was the greatest forgiver.

Christ lifts!

May each of us pledge to have our eyes a little more open, our hearts a little more willing, and our hands a little stronger to lift those around us in need.

My own journey through life has been rife with mistakes, second chances, and more failures than successes. But as sure as I know my weaknesses, I also know that if I'll *see* more, *love* more, and *lift* more, I will become *more* like Him.

And if that's true for me, it's certainly true for you.

Let's end where we began. Why am I writing this? Perhaps so we can share in our journeys together.

Cheer each other on. Share our successes, our failures, our good days and bad.

And maybe because the seeing, loving, and lifting will be so much easier if we come together and do it as one.

Together.

People Who Have

Seen, Loved, and *Lifted* Me

_____

_____

_____

_____

_____

_____

_____

_____

_____

_____

_____

_____

_____

_____

_____

_____

People I Will Learn to Better

See, Love, and Lift

_____

_____

_____

_____

_____

_____

_____

_____

_____

_____

_____

_____

_____

_____

_____

Meet Jason

Jason Wright is a *New York Times*, *Wall Street Journal* and *USA Today* best-selling author of Christmas Jars, The Wednesday Letters, and many others.

Christmas Jars was released as a Fathom Event feature film in 2019 and is now available on Apple TV and on various streaming services.

The Wednesday Letters is also in active film development and several others are in earlier stages.

His future projects include a novel, *The Bus to Gulf Breeze*, and a nonfiction project, *The Art of Mending Fences*.

Jason also contributes regularly to the opinion page on FoxNews.com and his hometown newspaper, *The Northern Virginia Daily.*

Hundreds of his columns have appeared in over 100 newspapers, magazines and web sites across the United States including *The Washington Times, The Chicago Tribune, and Forbes.*

Jason is also a popular speaker who speaks on the miracle of opening doors, faith, forgiveness, failure, the Christmas Jars movement, the lost art of letter writing, and many other topics.

Each year Jason also visits schools across the country and presents assemblies and writing workshops to students at all ages.

Information on booking Jason for speaking engagements, school visits, and workshops is available on his web site.

Jason has been seen by millions on CNN, FoxNews, C-SPAN, and on dozens of local television stations around the country.

Video clips of his appearances and highlights reels can be found on his website, Facebook, and Instagram.

Jason grew up in Charlottesville, Virginia, but has also lived in Germany, Illinois, Brazil, Oregon and Utah.

In 2007, while researching Virginia's Shenandoah Valley for his novel *The Wednesday Letters*, Jason fell so in love with the area that he moved his family an hour westward from northern Virginia to Woodstock.

Jason is married to the perfectly fabulous Kodi Erekson Wright and they have four wonderful children. Oakli, Jadi, Kason, and Koleson are doing their best to make their dad gray while simultaneously making a difference in the world. They also claim a son-in-law they quite like, Troy

Van Meter, and two grandchildren they like even more, Gary and Annie.

To connect with Jason, please visit him online or write to him the old-fashioned way. He responds (eventually!) to every single letter he receives.

www.jasonfwright.com
www.facebook.com/jfwbooks
www.instagram.com/jasonfwright

jason@jasonfwright.com

Jason Wright
Post Office Box 669
Woodstock, Virginia 22664

Made in the USA
Middletown, DE
07 December 2020

26630483R00050